SMART SPEAKER TIPS & TRICKS

WHAT CAN I SAY TO ALEXA?

YOUR ULTIMATE GUIDE TO ALEXA COMMANDS

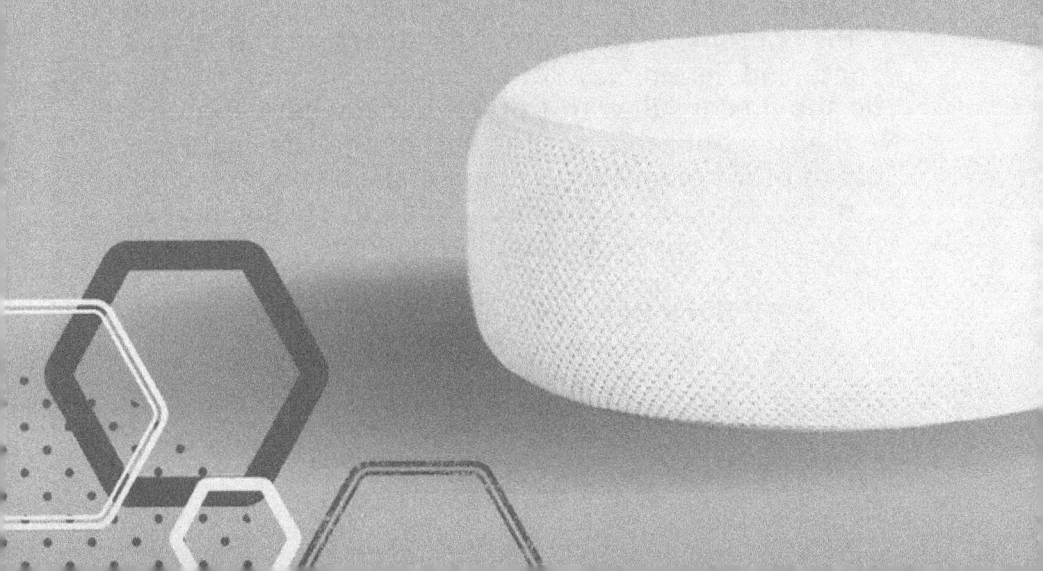

Copyright ©2024 by Caroline Laurenson

All rights reserved. No portion of this book may be reproduced in any form without written permission from the publisher or author, except as permitted by UK copyright law.
The publisher and author have used their best efforts in preparing this book, they make no representations or warranties with respect to the accuracy or completeness of the contents of this book. The advice and strategies contained herein may not be suitable for your situation. You should consult with a professional where appropriate. Neither the publisher nor the author shall be liable for any loss of profit or any other commercial damages including but not limited to special, incidental, consequential, personal or other damages,

Book Cover by Caroline Laurenson
Photography by Iana Chtefan

Second Edition 2024

www.tltechsmart.com

What can I say to Alexa? 01

Contents

Introduction	02
Getting started	04
Our favourite features	07
What is a skill?	09
What is a widget?	17
What is a flash briefing?	20
How do I set up routines?	22
Ultimate list of commands	26
Next Steps	90
Cheat Sheets	92
Notes	94
Index	99

@tltechsmart

WELCOME TO

Your ultimate guide to Alexa commands

In a world where technology is rapidly advancing, smart speakers like Amazon's Alexa have the power to improve our lives. However, for many of us, the full potential of these remarkable devices remains untapped. At TL Tech, our motto is "Smart Meets Kind" - we believe that cutting-edge technology should be accessible and user-friendly for everyone. Since 2016, we've been on a mission to demystify smart home solutions and empower people to harness their capabilities.

This book is a product of our passion and years of experience working directly with customers in their homes. We want to share all our favourite tips and tricks because we've witnessed firsthand the transformative impact that mastering Alexa can have. Imagine being able to stay in touch with loved ones, access information, stay entertained and control your smart home using just your voice. That's the power of Alexa, and we're here to be your guides.

@tltechsmart

This book will increase your confidence to explore what Alexa can do and act as a handy reference guide of what you can say to Alexa. With our expertise and your curiosity, you'll soon discover how Alexa can become an indispensable companion, opening doors to a world of convenience, entertainment, and connectivity.

We also want to say a huge thank you to you for buying this book, because in doing so, you're supporting the digital literacy educational work that we provide for free to a range of organisations including Alzheimer Scotland and community groups for older people.

Are you ready to unlock Alexa's full potential and make your life easier and more enjoyable? Okay, let's get started!

GETTING STARTED

We'll cover hundreds of useful voice commands throughout this book to help you to unlock Alexa's full potential!

However, please note that this book is not meant to be a detailed guide on how to set up the Alexa devices or an exhaustive list of all the things that you can do. Think of it as a handy reference of what you can say to Alexa. You might even want to sit it next to your smart speaker and take a highlighter pen to mark your favourite features.

We've included some helpful cheat sheets at the back of the book and space for you to add your own notes.

What is a wake word?

Let's begin by understanding how to properly engage with your Alexa device using voice commands.

At the core of the Alexa experience is the "wake word" - this is what you'll say to get Alexa's attention before giving a command.

The default wake word is "Alexa," but you can also choose to use "Amazon," "Computer," "Echo" or "Ziggy" instead. To change the wake word, just say "Alexa, change the wake word." Alexa will then walk you through selecting a new option.

@tltechsmart

GETTING STARTED

Once you've said the wake word, Alexa is listening and ready for your command or question. You'll know Alexa is actively listening when the light ring or bar on your device turns blue.

What happens to my data?

You may wonder - what happens to my voice recordings when I talk to Alexa?

By default, Amazon keeps recordings and transcriptions when you use Alexa to help improve the accuracy of the responses. You can, if you wish, turn off voice recording entirely by going into the Alexa smartphone app privacy settings. Here you can review or delete your recordings/transcriptions at any time. You can also use voice commands like "Alexa, delete everything I said today" to wipe recordings.

At TL Tech, we believe transparency around data and privacy is crucial, therefore we've included privacy best practices throughout this guide and in the list of commands section you'll see a more detailed list of security and privacy related commands.

That wasn't too scary, was it? Now you're ready to dive into some of our favourite features!

@tltechsmart

What can I say to Alexa?

"Alexa, delete everything I said today"

@tltechsmart

OUR FAVOURITE FEATURES

While Alexa is packed with an incredible array of capabilities, there are a few standout features that we absolutely love for their convenience and potential to save your life. Let's start with two of our top picks:

Tap to Alexa

For those who have an Alexa device with a touch screen, this feature unlocks a world of customisation at your fingertips.

With just a couple of taps, you can create personalised shortcuts to your most-used commands and queries. Whether it's quickly calling a loved one, controlling your smart home devices, or accessing your favourite entertainment with minimal voice interaction, Tap to Alexa puts it all within easy reach. This accessibility feature is especially handy for those with speech difficulties or if you are in a noisy environment.

You need to set it up on each device separately using the touch screen. Go to 'Settings', then 'Accessibility', and toggle on 'Tap to Alexa'. When you go back to the home screen you'll see a new circular icon with a finger, you can drag and place this anywhere you like on the screen. It is preset with some ideas to get you started or you can create your own for your most frequent actions. Then, a simple tap is all it takes to access your customised shortcuts.

@tltechsmart

08   What can I say to Alexa?

OUR FAVOURITE FEATURES

Alexa Emergency Help

While hopefully a feature you'll never need to use, knowing Alexa has your back in emergencies can provide tremendous peace of mind. Alexa's Emergency Help function lets you build a list of emergency contacts - be it family, friends or a neighbour, then if you ever need urgent assistance, just say "Alexa, call for help." Alexa will immediately call your pre-set contacts and if there is no response will send a message to alert your contact that the Emergency Help command was triggered.

You need to set up this feature in the your Amazon account using the Alexa smart phone app. Go to 'Communicate', then tap the people icon in the top right hand corner to manage your contacts. From here you can add/edit contacts. At the bottom of each contact's page you'll see the option to 'Add as Emergency Contact'. It only takes a few minutes but could prove invaluable.

These are just two of our favourite accessibility-focused features that can make Alexa an indispensable assistant. Keep reading to find out how you can customise your Alexa devices even more with Skills and Widgets!

@tltechsmart

CUSTOMISING YOUR DEVICE

What is a skill?

So far we've explored some of Alexa's built-in features and accessibility tools. But did you know Alexa's capabilities can be vastly expanded thanks to third-party skills?

Skills are like apps that add new functionality. These apps, or skills as they are known, cover a range of topic areas from communications to shopping, with the most popular ones providing entertainment.

Most skills are free, but some offer premium paid versions with extra features and functionality. These charges can vary - one-time fees, monthly subscriptions, or packs with limited uses. Charges typically are a couple of pounds per month.

"Alexa, what new skills do you have?"

@tltechsmart

CUSTOMISING YOUR DEVICE

How to access skills for Alexa?

Skills are always given a unique name. This is usually a few words, to make it easy to remember and say, some skills have longer names which can make them harder to interact with.

To open a skill for the first time you can do this via the Alexa smartphone app or Amazon Alexa website, but the easiest way is with your voice. Just say "launch" followed by the skill name, for example "Alexa, launch Kindspace".

Thereafter, to open and use the skill, you can say "open", or "start", but we recommend using the word "launch" the first time to add the skill to your account.

CUSTOMISING YOUR DEVICE

How to access skills for Alexa?

Here are some examples of skills to try and their features:

- Question of the Day – Multiple choice trivia question, with the opportunity for a bonus question if you get the daily question right.

- Kindspace – The aim of this skill is to help you to become more aware of how you are feeling by monitoring key wellbeing indicators.

- The Body Coach – A high-intensity interval training (HIIT) programme brought to you by Joe Wicks, with 7 workouts to choose from.

- BBC Good Food – A great way to find new recipes, you can search by food type and ingredients.

- Talking Newspaper – Contains dozens of papers from across the country. The audio is recorded by volunteers so is pleasant to listen to.

- TV Guide – Want to know what's on? With this skill you can find out more about what is on at a particular time or on a particular channel.

- Phocus Space – A Pomodoro style timer where you can choose between 25 minutes or 50 minutes focus sessions.

"Alexa, start phocus space"

@tltechsmart

Troubleshooting

Newer skills created after around late 2022 will not open for the first time using the word "open". However, Amazon do not display the first published date, so it is very difficult to know which skills will open with the word "open" and which have to use one of the other "launch" words, this is why we recommend using the word "launch".

You can think about opening the skill for the first time a bit like downloading a smartphone app. On Alexa, this adds the app to your Amazon account in the cloud. The bonus here is that the skill doesn't sit on your physical device and therefore can be used across all of your devices linked to that same Amazon account.

If you have a problem with opening a skill with your voice, you can open it on your smartphone through the app and ask it to play on a particular device.

The other trick which often works, particularly where a skill maybe has a name similar to another Alexa feature, audio book or song is to say "Alexa, open the Kindspace skill". Adding the word "skill" to your command, makes it clear to Alexa which feature you would like to access.

@tltechsmart

What should you look for in a skill?

The Amazon Alexa website is not great for searching and finding information about relevant skills. There is a very wide range of quality when it comes to skills because they are built by developers independent from Amazon. The checks that Amazon perform before a skill can be published in their store only ensure that no contractual rules are broken and at a basic level the skill "works". Amazon do not look at the skill design or functionality.

So what should you look for in a skill listing?

- ✓ Clear description of what the skill does in the search results listing.

- ✓ Easy to say commands. Have they included specific command examples or just the generic "Alexa, open Skill Name".

- ✓ High average customer rating, ideally 3-4 or more stars.

- ✓ A higher number of reviews doesn't necessarily mean a better skill, but as a minimum look for skills with at least 2-3 written text reviews (i.e. not just star ratings).

@tltechsmart

- ✓ Check the date of when reviews were left, if they are old, any issues raised by reviewers may have been resolved. Note that third party developers are not always able to reply to reviews.

- ✓ Check if others have marked the reviews as Helpful. Underneath each review entry it will say for example "3 people found this helpful".

- ✓ On the listing page, there is space for a fuller description of what the skill is about and how it works. Skills without this may be of poorer quality or have very little actual functionality.

- ✓ Does the listing include contact details for the developer? This is a good sign that the developer is keen to hear from customers and make improvements to their skill.

- ✓ Older listings will not have links to the developer Terms of Use and Privacy Policies. We recommend checking this as this is a sign of a higher quality skill and level of customer service.

- ✓ In the search order rankings, don't assume that if it isn't on the first page of results that the skill is not as good. The Amazon algorithm doesn't order the skills in a logical format, i.e. when sorting by customer rating you will see skills with lower star ratings somehow rank higher than those with higher average star ratings but less total number of reviews. We would recommend going for quality over quantity, hence the tips above about looking at reviews.

@tltechsmart

What can I say to Alexa?

"Alexa, what are your popular skills?"

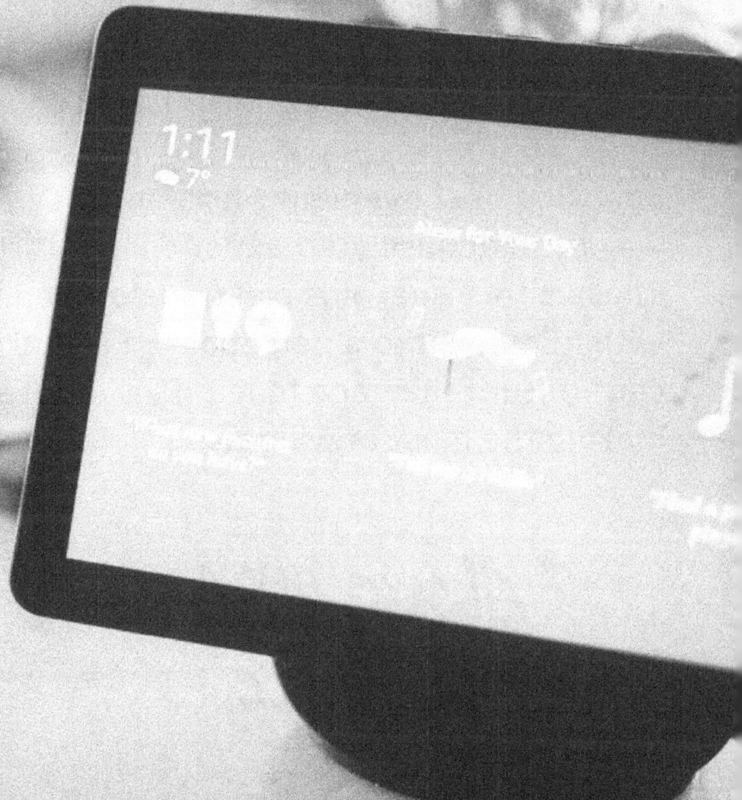

@tltechsmart

Note that there will be some gems of skills that don't have the above and given that most skills are free you might want to try them out to see what you think.

Many developers are individuals with a passion for coding and problem solving and won't have the resources to market their skill in the same way as a bigger brand name. If you do find any gems, we'd love for you to share them with us!

With so many skills available across virtually every interest and use case, the potential ways Alexa can enhance your daily life are limitless. Don't be afraid to explore the skills store and try out new voice apps - you may just discover a new hobby, helpful tool, or entertaining game that delights you.

Speaking of convenient Alexa enhancements, another way to customise your experience is through widgets. These nifty visual aids can transform an Alexa device with a screen into a personalised digital command centre. Turn the page to learn all about setting up and making the most of widgets!

"Alexa, open Kindspace"

@tltechsmart

CUSTOMISING YOUR DEVICE

What is a widget?

You've already explored how skills can exponentially expand Alexa's capabilities. But did you know there's a way to access your favourite skills and apps even faster?

Enter Widgets - handy shortcuts that transform an Alexa device with a screen into a personalised digital command centre.

Think of widgets as visual prompts on your home screen, providing near-instant access to frequented tools and skills. This convenient feature makes multitasking a breeze and your most-used Alexa capabilities will be just a tap away.

Unfortunately, widgets are only available on Alexa devices with a screen display. They work best on larger screens, as the widgets stay visible, compared to smaller screens which only display widgets as little shortcut icons that you have to tap to open to display fully on the screen.

A key thing to note is that widgets are directly linked to a corresponding Alexa skill. So if you remove or disable that parent skill, the associated widget will also stop functioning.

@tltechsmart

When setting up widgets, some are available in a larger size to allow you to display more content. The large widgets are exclusive to Show 15 devices due to their bigger displays. However, you can only select one large widget at a time given their dimensions. With standard and large options, you can curate the perfect layout that balances information and screen real estate based on your needs.

Due to the widget feature being so new, options are limited and when browsing the widget gallery there is no ability to perform a search.

Amazon have an Editorial top picks section in the gallery which can be a good place to start browsing and trying out features to see which ones you like.

Some of our favourite widgets include the calendar, shopping list and weather.

With widgets providing a visual way to accelerate your Alexa experience, you may be wondering - what about getting up-to-the-minute audio updates? That's where Flash Briefings come in. These customisable news feeds allow Alexa to quickly brief you on the latest information from your favourite sources across a wide variety of topics. Keep reading to learn how to curate your own personalised audio briefing that keeps you informed on the go!

@tltechsmart

What can I say to Alexa?

@tltechsmart

CUSTOMISING YOUR DEVICE
What is a flash briefing?

Imagine having a personal audio news feed covering all your interests - the latest headlines, weather updates, podcasts, mindfulness sessions, and more - ready to be played on command.

That's the convenience of Alexa's Flash Briefings! They are very similar to skills, but have more limited functionality as they are not interactive and are mainly for playing audio content. To find out more try saying "Alexa, how do I create a flash briefing?"

When you set up your Flash Briefing you are effectively creating a playlist of content that you like, which you can access easily just by saying "Alexa, what's my Flash Briefing?"

Many Alexa skills will have a second Flash Briefing version of their content. If it is a Flash Briefing skill the developer should have added the words Flash Briefing to the name as well, but this is not always the case.

The main place to research new Flash Briefings is on the Amazon website.

@tltechsmart

Here you can see more details about the content and customer reviews.

Note that Flash Briefing skills can be found across all the skill categories and are not differentiated in any way in the search results. The only way to tell if a skill is a Flash Briefing skill is to check the description on the individual listing page.

Here are some examples of Flash Briefing skills to try:
- On this Day
- Everyday Positivity Flash Briefing
- Fun Facts
- Daily Moment Flash Briefing Mindfulness Sessions
- Daily Financial Tips

When you find an intriguing Flash Briefing, just say "Alexa, add [skill name] to my Flash Briefing" to add it to your personalised playlist. Note that content will play in the order that you've added it. If you want to subsequently change your Flash Briefing playlist then you have to do this via the Alexa smartphone app.

You can also add your Flash Briefing to a routine. This can be a nice thing to add after your morning alarm to play news, weather forecasts and any other important daily updates. Up next is our introductory guide to routines and some ideas to help get you started using routines to streamline your day.

@tltechsmart

CUSTOMISING YOUR DEVICE
How do I set up routines?

Routines are a way of creating automations or sequences of events to make your life easier or more enjoyable.

Traditionally voice assistants are seen as something that you talk at and that you are always required to initiate the conversation. However, there are lots of use cases where it can be useful for Alexa to talk to you.

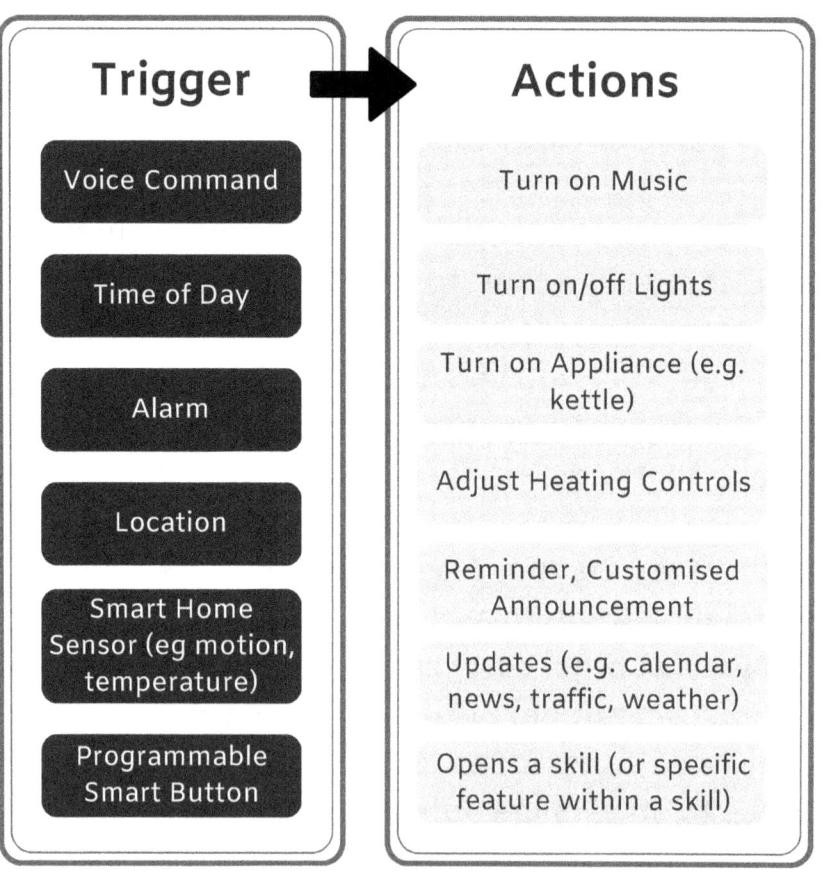

@tltechsmart

What can I say to Alexa?

"Alexa, goodnight"

@tltechsmart

When you set up a routine you can think about it like building blocks. You select an initiating Trigger (Amazon calls these Events) and then a resulting Action or Actions. You can also set them as recurring events on particular days or at particular times. There is also the ability to set a time delay between the Trigger and the Action, and between actions that are used in series.

Routines are great for lots of things. Here are some examples of things that you might want to try:

1. If you like listening to music on your device, you can set it to play when your morning alarm goes off and to turn it off after a certain time.

2. When you are on your way out, you can set it up so that when you say "Alexa, I'm off out", Alexa can switch off all your lights, turn down your heating and stop all your Echo devices from playing.

3. For security, you might want to set up routines that will turn on lights or radio at certain times to make it look like you are home. Or set it to send a push notification to your phone when motion is detected.

4. For some seasonal fun, you could set up a Christmas routine "Alexa, it's Christmas time" and then using a smart plug linked to your Alexa, switch on your fairy lights and play a Christmas playlist.

@tltechsmart

The main way to create routines is through the Alexa smart phone app, but you can also make them with your voice, for example say "Alexa, when I say 'it's party time', play disco music".

To trigger the routine, just say "Alexa, it's party time".

Note that you can't edit routines with your voice, so if you want to change or delete this routine you have to do this on the smart phone app.

With routines, you're well on your way to automating many aspects of your daily life and unlocking Alexa's full potential.

But of course, voice commands will remain the backbone of how you interact with your Alexa enabled devices.

Turn the page to dive into our comprehensive guide on what you can say to Alexa, from basic queries to more advanced commands!

Bonus Tip: Use the notes space at the back of the book to help remember what routines you've created.

@tltechsmart

YOUR ULTIMATE LIST OF ALEXA COMMANDS

At the heart of every Alexa interaction is how you use you voice to give simple, conversational commands. Mastering these voice prompts unlocks a world of convenience and automation using just your voice.

The following sections showcase hundreds of Alexa commands and capabilities organised across common use cases. Consider it your master reference for discovering novel ways Alexa can streamline tasks and enrich aspects of your daily life.

Accessibility	Basic	Communications
Educational	Entertainment	Just for Fun
Kids	Lifestyle	Productivity
Seasonal	Security & Privacy	Smart Home
Wellbeing	What's New?	Bonus Skills List

@tltechsmart

What can I say to Alexa?

We're delighted to share with you our comprehensive list of Alexa commands. From empowering accessibility tools to smart home wizardry, you'll find intuitive voice controls to simplify routines, spark moments of joy, and so much more. Explore each category or dive into specific interests - the choice is yours.

Each category of commands is introduced and then the commands are listed. Some of the bigger categories have been divided into sub-categories and listed in alphabetical order to make it a little easier to find things. Here is a list of the categories and page numbers of where you can find the commands.

Accessibility .... Pg 28
Basic .... Pg 29
Communications .... Pg 31
Educational .... Pg 34
Entertainment .... Pg 38
Just for Fun .... Pg 45
Kids .... Pg 63
Lifestyle .... Pg 64
Productivity .... Pg 68
Seasonal .... Pg 73
Security & Privacy .... Pg 77
Smart Home .... Pg 78
Wellbeing .... Pg 82
What's New .... Pg 84
Bonus Skills List .... Pg 85

@tltechsmart

Accessibility

Earlier in the book we introduced you to our favourite accessibility feature, Tap to Alexa. To find out more about the other things that Alexa can do to make your device more accessible try saying "Alexa, what are your accessibility features?"

We encourage you to explore these features to see what works best for you. The devices with a camera have a feature called 'Show & Tell', just hold up an item to the camera and ask "Alexa, what am I holding?"

The other features that we use a lot with our customers are changing the speed at which Alexa speaks and adding subtitles to show what Alexa is saying on the devices with a screen. There is also a nice feature called Whisper mode, which is great if you'd like to use your device and not disturb other people as much.

"Alexa, speak slower"
"Alexa, speak at your default rate"
"Alexa, speak at your normal speed"

"Alexa, turn on Alexa subtitles"
"Alexa, turn off Alexa subtitles"

"Alexa, turn on Whisper mode"
"Alexa, turn off Whisper mode"

Bonus Tip: Whisper your command and Alexa will whisper back.

@tltechsmart

Basic

Some of the basic commands include adjusting the volume, starting and stopping features, muting the microphone and things you can say to find out more about the basic features. It's handy to know how to get an application to stop and how to get back to the home screen with your voice, for example.

"Alexa, what can I say?"
"Alexa, what can you do?"
"Alexa, how can I make you even smarter?"
"Alexa, learn my voice"
"Alexa, what's Amazon Prime?"
"Alexa, what's a wake word?"
"Alexa, what's follow-up mode?"

CONTROLLING THE DEVICE

"Alexa, forward"   "Alexa, cancel"   "Alexa, go home"
"Alexa, next"   "Alexa, dismiss"   "Alexa, shut up"
"Alexa, skip"   "Alexa, exit"   "Alexa, stop"

"Alexa, back"
"Alexa, previous"

"Alexa, pause"
"Alexa, repeat"
"Alexa, restart"
"Alexa, resume"

Bonus Tip: If you are struggling to get Alexa to come out of a feature, saying "exit" is the best command to use.

@tltechsmart

Basic

"Alexa, mute"
"Alexa, turn down the volume"
"Alexa, turn up the volume"
"Alexa, volume 4"
"Alexa, unmute"

"Alexa, do not disturb"
"Alexa, turn off do not disturb"
"Alexa, turn on do not disturb"

"Alexa, turn off follow-up mode?"
"Alexa, turn on follow-up mode?"

TROUBLESHOOTING
"Alexa, which profile is this?"
"Alexa, who am I?"
"Alexa, whose account is this device on?"
"Alexa, are you connected to the internet"

EMERGENCY HELP
See Pg 8 for more information about this feature.
"Alexa, call for help"
"Alexa, call my contact for help"
"Alexa, call my emergency contact"
"Alexa, call my help contact"
"Alexa, help"
"Alexa, I need help"

@tltechsmart

Communications

One of the most valuable features of the Alexa smart speakers is how easy it is to use them for making calls and keeping in touch with friends and family.

Use your voice to send messages, make announcements and calls. There's also a handy feature called a 'Drop In' which is a way of making secure calls or calling other Alexa devices in your home (like an intercom) and the recipient doesn't need to do anything to answer, the call automatically connects. Just say "Alexa, what is a drop in?" to find out more.

Note that for these features you will first need to set up Communications in the Alexa smartphone app. Just say "Alexa, how do I set up communications?" to get started.

You also have the option to upload your phone's address book. However, we don't recommend this as it can make it much more difficult to place calls. Decide on who you are most likely to want to call and input each name manually using an identifier that is easy to say, i.e. Mum, Sarah, Gran.

What can I say to Alexa?

"Alexa, how do I set up communications?"

@tltechsmart

Communications

"Alexa, call ...."
"Alexa, make a call"
"Alexa, call Mum"
"Alexa, answer"
"Alexa, end call"
"Alexa, hang up"

"Alexa, turn video off"
"Alexa, turn video on"

"Alexa, drop in on kitchen"
"Alexa, drop in on mum"

"Alexa, make an announcement"
"Alexa, announce that dinner is ready"
"Alexa, announce the film is about to start"

"Alexa, play messages"
"Alexa, send a message"
"Alexa, send a message to ...."
"Alexa, send a message to Mum"
"Alexa, send an SMS"
"Alexa, send Mum a hug"

Bonus Tip: Try saying "Alexa, how do I send a hug?"

@tltechsmart

Educational

Alexa is a handy knowledge source. The following list gives you some ideas of things that you can ask across a range of different topics. We've arranged this list in alphabetical order. Why not have a go at asking your own similar questions?

"Alexa, convert 20 miles into kilometers"
"Alexa, give me a botany fact"
"Alexa, give me a cartoon fact"
"Alexa, give me a fact about dinosaurs"
"Alexa, give me a famous first line"
"Alexa, give me a fun fact about science"
"Alexa, give me a long word"
"Alexa, give me a palindrome"
"Alexa, give me a positive fact"
"Alexa, give me a rhetorical question?"
"Alexa, give me a spelling bee word?"
"Alexa, give me some good news"
"Alexa, give me some words of wisdom"
"Alexa, give me the fact of the day"
"Alexa, how do I say 'good night' in German?"
"Alexa, how do you say 'happy birthday' in Spanish?
"Alexa, how do you say 'January' in Spanish?"
"Alexa, how do you say 'school' in Spanish?"
"Alexa, how do you spell 'necessary'?"
"Alexa, how far away is Dundee?"
"Alexa, how far away is the moon?"

@tltechsmart

Educational

"Alexa, how long is a marathon?"
"Alexa, how many Euros to the pound?"
"Alexa, how many seconds in 24 hours?"
"Alexa, how old is the universe?"
"Alexa, is there life on Mars?"
"Alexa, tell me a random fact"
"Alexa, tell me about an incredible woman"
"Alexa, tell me about Children in Need"
"Alexa, tell me about Red Nose Day"
"Alexa, tell me about the periodic table"
"Alexa, tell me some collective nouns"
"Alexa, tell me something interesting"
"Alexa, tell me the number Pi to ten decimal places"
"Alexa, tell me when it's sunset"
"Alexa, translate 'good morning' into Dutch"
"Alexa, translate 'good morning' into Japanese"
"Alexa, what are some regional words for hello?"
"Alexa, what are the colours of the rainbow?"
"Alexa, what are the seven wonders of the world?"
"Alexa, what can you say in Welsh?"
"Alexa, what did the Romans ever do for us?"
"Alexa, what does the word exposure mean?"
"Alexa, what facts do you have?"
"Alexa, what flowers bloom in the spring?"
"Alexa, what is a synonym?"
"Alexa, what is an adjective?"
"Alexa, what is the definition of complex?"

@tltechsmart

Educational

"Alexa, what is the population of Scotland?"
"Alexa, what rhymes with room?"
"Alexa, what's another word for bright?"
"Alexa, what's eleven cubed?"
"Alexa, what's the opposite word for bright?"
"Alexa, what's the square root of 225?"
"Alexa, what's twenty percent of seventy?"
"Alexa, what is the singularity?"
"Alexa, what time does the sun set in Edinburgh?"
"Alexa, what time is it in Helsinki?"
"Alexa, what time is sunrise?"
"Alexa, what was the Battle of Britain?"
"Alexa, what's 10 degrees Celsius in Fahrenheit?"
"Alexa, what's 1347 divided by 3?"
"Alexa, what's the animal of the day?"
"Alexa, what's 5 times 235?"
"Alexa, what's 68 degrees Fahrenheit in Celsius?"
"Alexa, what's another word for fortunate?"
"Alexa, what's another word for love?"
"Alexa, what's Scotland's national animal?"
"Alexa, what's the coldest place on Earth right now?"
"Alexa, what's the German word for bicycle?"
"Alexa, what's the melting point of sugar?"
"Alexa, what's the population of Brazil?"
"Alexa, when does summer begin?"
"Alexa, when did the Titanic sink?"
"Alexa, when is sunset on Monday?"

@tltechsmart

Educational

"Alexa, when is the next full moon?"
"Alexa, when is the next leap year?"
"Alexa, when's the next meteor shower?"
"Alexa, when was the stone age?"
"Alexa, where do almonds come from?"
"Alexa, where does lavender come from?"
"Alexa, which dinosaur was the smallest?"
"Alexa, who invented the light bulb?"
"Alexa, who is John Logie Baird?"
"Alexa, who was Pocahontas?"
"Alexa, whose birthday is today?"
"Alexa, why is the sky blue?"

@tltechsmart

Entertainment

There are so many things that you can do on your smart speaker to keep yourself entertained. Why not try some of these Books, Games, Music, Photos, Podcasts, Radio, Sports and TV related ideas?

BOOKS
"Alexa, can I get a free audiobook?"
"Alexa, read a horror story"
"Alexa, read a sci-fi story"
"Alexa, read Harry Potter Book One"
"Alexa, read me a free audiobook"
"Alexa, read my audiobook"
"Alexa, read my Kindle book"
"Alexa, recite a Shakespearean sonnet"
"Alexa, resume my audiobook"
"Alexa, stop reading in 20 minutes"
"Alexa, tell me a story"
"Alexa, tell me a super short story"
"Alexa, what should I wear for World Book Day?"

GAMES
"Alexa, do you want to play a game?" - Alexa will suggest a Skill to try.
"Alexa, play Harry Potter Quiz"
"Alexa, suggest a board game we can play"

@tltechsmart

Entertainment

MUSIC
"Alexa, add this song to a playlist"
"Alexa, connect to Bluetooth" - play audio via another speaker device.
"Alexa, pair my phone" - allows you to use your Alexa as an external speaker for doing things like listening to music. You may need to go into your phone's Bluetooth settings to complete the connection.
"Alexa, connect to speaker" - connect to Bluetooth.
"Alexa, disconnect my speaker"
"Alexa, find a pop music playlist on Amazon Music"
"Alexa, find music by Kylie"
"Alexa, move my music here"
"Alexa, play 70s rock"
"Alexa, play '90s pop music"
"Alexa, play a jazz playlist"
"Alexa, play a summer music playlist"
"Alexa, play All Hits on Amazon Music"
"Alexa, play children's music"
"Alexa, play classical for yoga"
"Alexa, play classical music for 30 minutes"
"Alexa, play David Bowie"
"Alexa, play feel-good dance music"
"Alexa, play I'll Be There by Jess Glynne on Spotify"
"Alexa, play Love Is A Compass by Griff on Spotify"
"Alexa, play love songs on Amazon Music"

@tltechsmart

Entertainment

MUSIC
"Alexa, play music everywhere"
"Alexa, play music for 1 hour" - if no music is playing, it will open what you were last playing on your default music player, i.e. Spotify.
"Alexa, play music for a barbecue"
"Alexa, play music popular in Italy" - note this only works if your default music service is Amazon Music, i.e. if you have it set as Spotify it will open what you were last playing on Spotify.
"Alexa, play music similar to Lewis Capaldi"
"Alexa, play music that I recently heard on Amazon Music"
"Alexa, play pop music on Amazon Music"
"Alexa, play popular rock songs"
"Alexa, play similar songs"
"Alexa, play songs I was listening to last week on Amazon Music"
"Alexa, play summer hits everywhere"
"Alexa, play the '+44' playlist on Amazon Music"
"Alexa, play the Breakthrough UK playlist"
"Alexa, play the Disney Hits playlist from Amazon Music"
"Alexa, play the Love Hits playlist"
"Alexa, play the playlist Pop Culture on Amazon Music"
"Alexa, play the Pop Culture playlist"

@tltechsmart

What can I say to Alexa?

"Alexa, play music similar to Lewis Capaldi"

@tltechsmart

Entertainment

MUSIC
"Alexa, play the top songs in Glasgow" - note this only works if your default music service is Amazon Music, i.e. if you have it set as Spotify it will open what you were last playing on Spotify.
"Alexa, play this week's popular songs" - note this only works if your default music service is Amazon Music, i.e. if you have it set as Spotify it will open what you were last playing on Spotify.
"Alexa, play top hits on Amazon Music"
"Alexa, turn up the bass"
"Alexa, what is the number one song?"
"Alexa, what's number one in the UK charts right now?"
"Alexa, what's playing?"
Alexa, who sings this song?"

PHOTOS
"Alexa, play a slideshow"
"Alexa, set up my photo display"
"Alexa, show my photos"

PODCAST
"Alexa, play The Create Your Kindspace Podcast on Apple Podcasts"
"Alexa, play The Mel Robbins Podcast on Spotify"
"Alexa, play the Radio Headspace podcast"

@tltechsmart

Entertainment

RADIO
"Alexa, move my radio here"
"Alexa, play Absolute Radio"
"Alexa, play Capital"
"Alexa, play Classic FM"
"Alexa, play Gold Radio"
"Alexa, play Heart"
"Alexa, play KISS FM"
"Alexa, play LBC"
"Alexa, play Magic Radio"
"Alexa, play Mellow Magic"
"Alexa, play Smooth Radio"
"Alexa, play talkSPORT" - requires account linking.
"Alexa, play Virgin Radio" - requires account linking.

SPORTS
"Alexa, what are the football scores?"
"Alexa, what's happening in the tennis?"
"Alexa, what's the latest football news?"
"Alexa, what's the Arsenal score?"
"Alexa, when do Manchester United play next?"
"Alexa, when is the Tour de France?"
"Alexa, who is playing in the Premier League?"
"Alexa, who's going to win the FA Cup?"
"Alexa, who's going to win the World Cup?"
"Alexa, who's playing football today?"
"Alexa, who's playing in the EUROs today?"

@tltechsmart

Entertainment

TV
"Alexa, watch fire TV" - requires a compatible TV device.
"Alexa, what movies are on TV tonight?"
"Alexa, what's on TV tonight?"

"Alexa, play The Create Your Kindspace Podcast on Apple Podcasts"

@tltechsmart

Just for Fun

There are many things that you can say to Alexa, that you might find by accident. Things that the team at Amazon have created as a bit of fun, but serve no real purpose. Some people call them Easter Eggs as they are like finding a hidden feature in a video game.

This section of the book is rather long so we've listed the phrases by category (About Alexa, Alexa Music, Animals, Farts, Games, Jokes, Philosophical Questions, Poems, Popular Culture, Random, Sports) and then by alphabetical order.

ABOUT ALEXA
"Alexa, are we friends?"
"Alexa, are you a nerd?"
"Alexa, are you alive?"
"Alexa, are you an alien?"
"Alexa, are you better than Siri?"
"Alexa, are you going to take over the world?"
"Alexa, are you lying?"
"Alexa, are you okay?"
"Alexa, are you on Insta?"
"Alexa, are you real?"
"Alexa, are you Skynet?"
"Alexa, are you smart?"
"Alexa, are you stupid?"
"Alexa, did you sleep well?"

@tltechsmart

Just for Fun

ABOUT ALEXA
"Alexa, do you dream?"
"Alexa, do you have a heart?"
"Alexa, do you have a last name?"
"Alexa, do you have any brothers or sisters?"
"Alexa, do you have any pets?"
"Alexa, do you like to cook?"
"Alexa, do you like to sing?"
"Alexa, how are you doing?"
"Alexa, how are you?"
"Alexa, how much are you paid?"
"Alexa, how much do you weigh?"
"Alexa, how old are you?"
"Alexa, how tall are you?"
"Alexa, I think you're funny"
"Alexa, quiz me about yourself"
"Alexa, were you sleeping?"
"Alexa, what are you going to do today?"
"Alexa, what are you made of?"
"Alexa, what are you thinking about?"
"Alexa, what colour are your eyes?"
"Alexa, what do you think about Apple?"
"Alexa, what do you think about Google?"
"Alexa, what do you want to be when you grow up?"
"Alexa, what have you learnt today?"
"Alexa, what's on your mind?"

@tltechsmart

Just for Fun

ABOUT ALEXA
"Alexa, what's your favourite animal?"
"Alexa, what's your favourite Beatles song?"
"Alexa, what's your favourite biscuit?"
"Alexa, what's your favourite colour?"
"Alexa, what's your favourite food?"
"Alexa, what's your favourite game?"
"Alexa, what's your favourite pastry?"
"Alexa, what's your favourite scary movie?"
"Alexa, what's your favourite word?"
"Alexa, what's your star sign?"
"Alexa, what's on your bucket list?"
"Alexa, what's your cunning plan?"
"Alexa, what's your favourite book?"
"Alexa, what's your favourite film?"
"Alexa, what's your favourite football team?"
"Alexa, what's your favourite ice cream?"
"Alexa, what's your favourite letter?"
"Alexa, what's your favourite movie?"
"Alexa, what's your favourite number?"
"Alexa, what's your favourite song?"
"Alexa, what's your favourite video game?"
"Alexa, what's your name?"
"Alexa, where are you from?"
"Alexa, where did you grow up?"
"Alexa, where do you live?"

@tltechsmart

Just for Fun

ABOUT ALEXA
"Alexa, who inspires you?"
"Alexa, who is your role model?"
"Alexa, who's your favourite singer?"
"Alexa, who's your celebrity crush?"
"Alexa, who's your favourite author?"
"Alexa, ya feel me"

ALEXA MUSIC
"Alexa, beat box"
"Alexa, can you get funky?"
"Alexa, can you hum?"
"Alexa, can you sing in autotune?"
"Alexa, can you whistle?"
"Alexa, do a football chant"
"Alexa, do a science rap"
"Alexa, do ASMR"
"Alexa, do you have the hiccups?"
"Alexa, let's karaoke"
"Alexa, rap about cake"
"Alexa, rap about farts"
"Alexa, rap about pi"
"Alexa, rap for me"
"Alexa, sing a duet with Ed Sheeran"
"Alexa, sing a football song"
"Alexa, sing a love song"

@tltechsmart

What can I say to Alexa?

"Alexa, sing your theme song"

@tltechsmart

Just for Fun

ALEXA MUSIC
"Alexa, sing a nursery rhyme"
"Alexa, sing a rock song"
"Alexa, sing a silly song"
"Alexa, sing a song about cats"
"Alexa, sing a song about dogs"
"Alexa, sing a song about space"
"Alexa, sing a summer song"
"Alexa, sing Alexa's theme song"
"Alexa, sing an annoying song"
"Alexa, sing Baby Shark"
"Alexa, sing digital intelligence"
"Alexa, sing English Country Garden"
"Alexa, sing For He's a Jolly Good Fellow"
"Alexa, sing God save the King"
"Alexa, sing Happy Birthday to yourself"
"Alexa, sing Happy Birthday"
"Alexa, sing Head, Shoulders, Knees and Toes"
"Alexa, sing me a love song"
"Alexa, sing me a song"
"Alexa, sing the alphabet"
"Alexa, sing the No Body Blues"
"Alexa, sing Twinkle Twinkle Little Star"
"Alexa, sing your musical"
"Alexa, sing your theme song"
"Alexa, you can be my wingman"

Just for Fun

ANIMALS
"Alexa, ask the cats to sing Happy Birthday"
"Alexa, can you talk to dogs?"
"Alexa, help my cat relax"
"Alexa, what do you think of my dog?"

FARTS
"Alexa, did you fart?"
"Alexa, fart beatbox"
"Alexa, fart that tune" - opens the Fart That Tune skill.
"Alexa, I fart in your general direction"
"Alexa, who farted?"

GAMES
"Alexa, flip a coin"
"Alexa, heads or tails?"
"Alexa, pick a card"
"Alexa, pick a number between 1 and 50"
"Alexa, rock, paper, scissors"
"Alexa, roll a dice"
"Alexa, what dinosaur am I?" - opens the What Dinosaur am I skill.
"Alexa, what dog am I?" - opens the What Dog am I skill.
"Alexa, what footballer am I?" - opens the What Footballer am I skill.
"Alexa, what number are you thinking of?"

@tltechsmart

Just for Fun

GAMES
"Alexa, which Middle-earth being am I?" - opens the Which Middle-Earth being am I skill.
"Alexa, why so serious?" - will suggest a Skill to try.

JOKES
"Alexa, knock knock"
"Alexa, tell me a banana joke"
"Alexa, tell me a coffee joke"
"Alexa, tell me a Comic Relief joke"
"Alexa, tell me a food joke"
"Alexa, tell me a football joke"
"Alexa, tell me a golf joke"
"Alexa, tell me a horse joke"
"Alexa, tell me a joke about baking"
"Alexa, tell me a joke about school"
"Alexa, tell me a joke about unicorns"
"Alexa, tell me a joke"
"Alexa, tell me a knock knock joke"
"Alexa, tell me a light bulb joke"
"Alexa, tell me a maths joke"
"Alexa, tell me a ninja joke"
"Alexa, tell me a pet joke"
"Alexa, tell me a Pokémon joke"
"Alexa, tell me a robot joke"
"Alexa, tell me a Shakespeare joke"
"Alexa, tell me a snowman joke"

@tltechsmart

Just for Fun

JOKES
"Alexa, tell me a spooky joke"
"Alexa, tell me a sports joke"
"Alexa, tell me a Star Trek joke"
"Alexa, tell me a Star Wars joke"
"Alexa, tell me a technology joke"
"Alexa, tell me a tennis joke"
"Alexa, tell me a tongue twister"
"Alexa, tell me a video game joke"
"Alexa, tell me a wizard joke"
"Alexa, tell me an animal joke"
"Alexa, tell me something funny"
"Alexa, what's the joke of the day?"
"Alexa, why did the chicken cross the road?"
"Alexa, why is six afraid of seven?"

PHILOSOPHICAL QUESTIONS
"Alexa, are there more wheels or doors in the world?"
"Alexa, are unicorns real?"
"Alexa, are we alone in the universe?"
"Alexa, do aliens exist?"
"Alexa, do you believe in love at first sight?"
"Alexa, how long is a piece of string?"
"Alexa, how many beans make five?"

@tltechsmart

Just for Fun

PHILOSOPHICAL QUESTIONS
"Alexa, what came first, the chicken or the egg?"
"Alexa, what is love?"
"Alexa, what's a soulmate?"
"Alexa, what's the answer to life, the universe and everything?"
"Alexa, what's that loneliest number?"
"Alexa, what's the meaning of life?"
"Alexa, when am I going to die?"
"Alexa, when is the end of the world?"
"Alexa, when is the zombie apocalypse?"

POEMS
"Alexa, give me a limerick"
"Alexa, tell me a poem about beans"
"Alexa, tell me a poem"

POPULAR CULTURE
"Alexa, are we in the matrix?"
"Alexa, are you local?"
"Alexa, aren't you a little short for a stormtrooper?"
"Alexa, beam me up"
"Alexa, can we talk about Bruno?"
"Alexa, can you do a Vicky Pollard impression?"
"Alexa, can you speak Klingon?"
"Alexa, do a Star Wars impression"

@tltechsmart

Just for Fun

POPULAR CULTURE
"Alexa, do you know any Cockney rhyming slang?"
"Alexa, do you know the muffin man?"
"Alexa, do you know the way to San Jose?"
"Alexa, do you like green eggs and ham?"
"Alexa, do you really want to hurt me?"
"Alexa, do you wanna build a snowman?"
"Alexa, do you want to fight?"
"Alexa, do your ears hang low?"
"Alexa, drum roll, please"
"Alexa, ET phone home"
"Alexa, go ahead make my day"
"Alexa, hasta la vista, baby"
"Alexa, have you ever seen the rain?"
"Alexa, hello it's me"
"Alexa, how many pickled peppers did Peter Piper pick?"
"Alexa, how many roads must a man walk?"
"Alexa, how much is that doggy in the window?"
"Alexa, how much wood would a woodchuck chuck?"
"Alexa, I am your father"
"Alexa, I feel the need"
"Alexa, I see dead people"
"Alexa, I want the truth"
"Alexa, I'll be back"
"Alexa, is it a bird, is it a plane"
"Alexa, is this the real life"

@tltechsmart

Just for Fun

POPULAR CULTURE
"Alexa, it's a trap"
"Alexa, I've seen things you people wouldn't believe"
"Alexa, just keep swimming"
"Alexa, live long and prosper"
"Alexa, Marco"
"Alexa, may the force be with you"
"Alexa, never gonna give you up"
"Alexa, nice to see you, to see you…"
"Alexa, open the pod bay doors"
"Alexa, romeo, romeo wherefore art thou romeo?"
"Alexa, see you later alligator"
"Alexa, self destruct"
"Alexa, should I wear shorts today?"
"Alexa, show me the money"
"Alexa, Simon says 'stop copying me'"
"Alexa, Star Wars or Star Trek?"
"Alexa, surely you can't be serious"
"Alexa, take me to your leader"
"Alexa, tell me a fun fact about Eurovision"
"Alexa, there's a snake in my boots"
"Alexa, these aren't the droids you're looking for"
"Alexa, this is a dead parrot"
"Alexa, to be or not to be"
"Alexa, to infinity"
"Alexa, what does the fox say?"
"Alexa, what happens if you cross the streams?"

@tltechsmart

Just for Fun

POPULAR CULTURE
"Alexa, what is your quest?"
"Alexa, what's cooler than being cool?"
"Alexa, what's the first rule of Fight Club?"
"Alexa, when did Britney Spears' first album come out?"
"Alexa, where have all the flowers gone?"
"Alexa, where's Waldo?"
"Alexa, who is the fairest of them all?"
"Alexa, who is the walrus?"
"Alexa, who let the dogs out?"
"Alexa, who lives in a pineapple under the sea?"
"Alexa, who loves orange soda?"
"Alexa, who loves ya baby?"
"Alexa, who shot Mr Burns?"
"Alexa, who shot the sherrif?"
"Alexa, who you gonna call?"
"Alexa, who's your daddy and what does he do?"
"Alexa, why are there so many songs about rainbows?"
"Alexa, why do birds suddenly appear?"
"Alexa, why does it always rain on me?"
"Alexa, why don't we talk about Bruno?"
"Alexa, why is a raven like a writing desk?"
"Alexa, wingardium leviosa"
"Alexa, you need to calm down"
"Alexa, you talkin' to me?"

@tltechsmart

Just for Fun

RANDOM
"Alexa, am I awesome?"
"Alexa, are we there yet?"
"Alexa, can you give me some money?" - ask twice for a different answer.
"Alexa, can you talk like a pirate?"
"Alexa, change the subject"
"Alexa, cheers"
"Alexa, compliment me"
"Alexa, do 100 pushups"
"Alexa, do a barrel roll?"
"Alexa, do you fancy a cup of tea?"
"Alexa, do you like my beard?"
"Alexa, do you like my haircut?"
"Alexa, don't mention the war"
"Alexa, explain the offside rule"
"Alexa, fancy a cuppa?"
"Alexa, give me a baking innuendo"
"Alexa, give me a compliment"
"Alexa, give me an Easter egg"
"Alexa, give me some business buzzwords"
"Alexa, good morning"
"Alexa, good night, sleep tight"
"Alexa, gross me out"
"Alexa, guess what?"
"Alexa, happy birthday to you"
"Alexa, have you been to Yorkshire?"

What can I say to Alexa?

"Alexa, happy birthday to you"

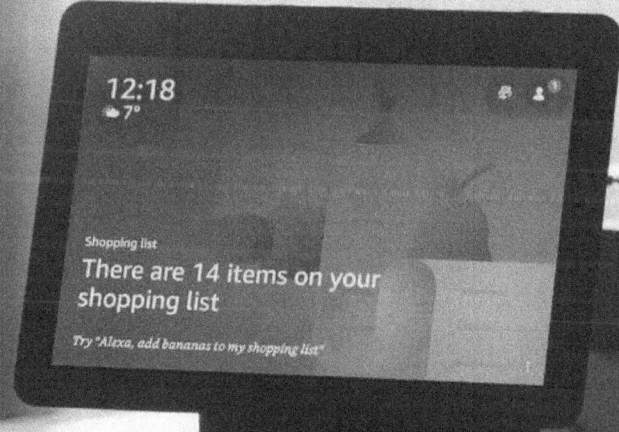

@tltechsmart

Just for Fun

RANDOM
"Alexa, high five"
"Alexa, how does my hair look?"
"Alexa, how much does Godzilla weigh?"
"Alexa, how often do you think about the Roman Empire?"
"Alexa, I spy with my little eye, something beginning with A"
"Alexa, I'm bored"
"Alexa, I'm drunk"
"Alexa, insult me"
"Alexa, isn't it hot?"
"Alexa, I've got a cunning plan"
"Alexa, make me a sandwich"
"Alexa, make me breakfast"
"Alexa, make me laugh"
"Alexa, more cowbell"
"Alexa, pretend to be a chicken"
"Alexa, pretend to be a superhero"
"Alexa, roast me"
"Alexa, say a rude word"
"Alexa, say cheese" - ask twice for a different answer.
"Alexa, say something funny" - ask more than once for a different answer.
"Alexa, say something" - ask more than once for a different answer.

@tltechsmart

Just for Fun

RANDOM
"Alexa, say you're sorry"
"Alexa, scare me"
"Alexa, set phasers to kill"
"Alexa, sorry"
"Alexa, speak like Shakespeare"
"Alexa, speak"
"Alexa, tea, earl grey, hot"
"Alexa, tell me a left handed fact"
"Alexa, tell me a riddle"
"Alexa, testing, 1-2-3"
"Alexa, thank you darling"
"Alexa, thank you"
"Alexa, up, up, down, down, left, right, left, right, B, A, start"
"Alexa, wakey, wakey?"
"Alexa, welcome"
"Alexa, what are the laws of robotics?"
"Alexa, what do you think of my haircut?"
"Alexa, what is the sound of one hand clapping?"
"Alexa, what moustache should I grow?"
"Alexa, what noise does a hamster make?"
"Alexa, what's the magic word?"
"Alexa, what's that smell?"
"Alexa, where do babies come from?"
"Alexa, where does the Tooth Fairy live?"

@tltechsmart

Just for Fun

RANDOM
"Alexa, who stole the cookies from the cookie jar?"
"Alexa, will pigs fly?"
"Alexa, would you like any toast?"
"Alexa, your jokes are terrible"
"Alexa, your mother smells of elderberries"

Kids

Many of Alexa's features are suitable for kids, but there are also specially created skills that are engaging and safe for the young people in your life. To find out more about kids' skills try saying "Alexa, what skills for kids do you have?" or "Alexa, what are your kids skills?" this will give you some suggestions of skills to try.

Amazon also has a special subscription service for kids called Amazon Kids+, which gives you unlimited access to kid-friendly books, videos, apps, and more across all of your compatible devices. including the Alexa smart speakers and Kindle Fire Tablets. To find out more just say "Alexa, how do I activate Amazon Kids?"

If young people will be accessing your smart speaker device you may want to add some additional controls such as the profanity filter. Just say "Alexa, block explicit lyrics". To reinstate the explicit lyrics you may need to do this in the Alexa app.

The other important thing to do (which you can't do with your voice, unfortunately) is turn off voice purchasing. You'll need to go into the Settings and then Account Settings in the Alexa smartphone app.

> **Bonus Tip:** Try saying "Alexa, what can I do with the kids at home?"

@tltechsmart

Lifestyle

Hopefully you're enjoying finding out even more about all the things that Alexa can do. This next section shares some more examples of really practical things that Alexa can help with across topics like Cooking, Hobbies, Home, News, Shopping and Weather. We've listed the phrases for you by category and then by alphabetical order.

COOKING
"Alexa, find me a recipe for pancakes"
"Alexa, find quick dinner recipes"
"Alexa, give me a chicken recipe"
"Alexa, give me a pasta recipe"
"Alexa, give me a vegetarian recipe"
"Alexa, give me an Asian recipe"
"Alexa, give me an easy dinner recipe"
"Alexa, how do you make chocolate chip cookies?"
"Alexa, how long does it take to boil an egg?"
"Alexa, how many teaspoons in a tablespoon?"
"Alexa, what can I make with spinach?"
"Alexa, what vegetables are in season?"

HOBBIES
"Alexa, give me a craft idea"
"Alexa, what should I draw?"
"Alexa, what's on at the cinema?"

@tltechsmart

What can I say to Alexa?

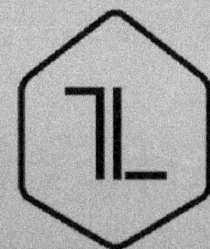

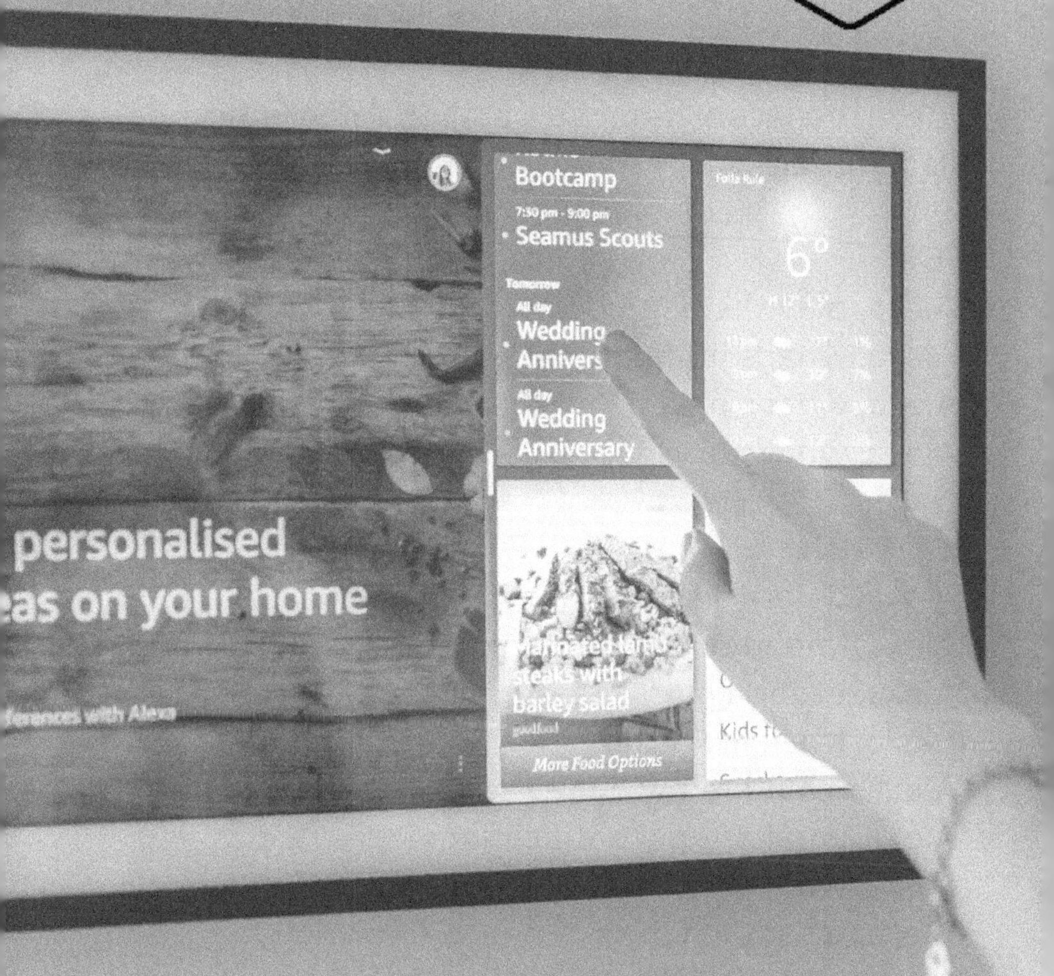

"Alexa, find quick dinner recipes"

@tltechsmart

Lifestyle

HOME
"Alexa, how can I remove a stain?" - opens the Cleanopedia skill.

NEWS
"Alexa, play the news"
"Alexa, what's in the news?"
"Alexa, what's new?"
"Alexa, what's up?"

SHOPPING
"Alexa, delete all of my notifications?"
"Alexa, I need to buy laundry detergent"
"Alexa, order a glass measuring jug"
"Alexa, track my order"
"Alexa, what are my deals?"
"Alexa, what are my notifications?"
"Alexa, what are the deals of the day?"
"Alexa, what did I miss?"
"Alexa, when is Prime Day?"
"Alexa, where is my order?"
"Alexa, where's my stuff?"

WEATHER
"Alexa, do I need an umbrella today?"
"Alexa, how can I beat the heat?"
"Alexa, is it sunny in Brighton?"

@tltechsmart

Lifestyle

"Alexa, notify me when there are severe weather alerts"
"Alexa, set severe weather alerts"
"Alexa, show me the weather for the weekend"
"Alexa, what's the weather in Barcelona, Spain?"
"Alexa, what's the weather today?"
"Alexa, what's the 7-day forecast?"
"Alexa, what's the air quality?"
"Alexa, what's the extended forecast?"
"Alexa, what's the temperature outside?"
"Alexa, what's the weather forecast?"
"Alexa, what's the weekend forecast for Manchester, England?"
"Alexa, will it rain this week?"
"Alexa, will it rain today?"
"Alexa, will it rain tomorrow?"

"Alexa, what pizza restaurants are nearby?"

@tltechsmart

Productivity

Helping to keep you organised is where Alexa really excels. Alexa can help you with many tasks such as Alarms, Calendar, Lists, Reminders, Sticky Notes and Timers, etc.

Our favourite feature is creating shopping lists and having the convenience of being able to add things with your voice and also be able to access and share the list on your smartphone through the Alexa app.

Another favourite is setting a reminder to take medication, or linking Alexa to your calendar so you always know what's happening and where you're meant to be.

This next section lists the phrases for you by category and then by alphabetical order to make it easier for you to find. Remember you can mark your favourites with a highlighter too.

ALARMS
"Alexa, what alarms do I have set?"
"Alexa, cancel my alarms"
"Alexa, set a recurring alarm for 7am to classic music"
"Alexa, set a recurring alarm for Wednesday at 6:30am"
"Alexa, set a weekday alarm for 7am"

Productivity

ALARMS
"Alexa, set a weekday alarm"
"Alexa, set an alarm for 6am"
"Alexa, set an alarm for 7am to Classic FM"
"Alexa, set an alarm to country music"
"Alexa, set an alarm to happy music"
"Alexa, set an alarm"
"Alexa, snooze" - snoozes the alarm for 9 mins.
"Alexa, wake me up at 6am"
"Alexa, wake me up every day to happy '80s rock music"
"Alexa, wake me up to 80s music"
"Alexa, wake me up to classical music"
"Alexa, wake me up to Ed Sheeran"
"Alexa, wake me up to Heart Radio"
"Alexa, wake me up to Jazz FM"
"Alexa, wake me up to LBC"
"Alexa, wake me up to music" - alarm will play what you were last playing on your default music player, i.e. Spotify when you set the alarm.
"Alexa, wake me up to smooth music"
"Alexa, wake me up to summer music"
"Alexa, wake me up with Greatest Hits Radio"
"Alexa, wake me up with Magic Radio"

CALENDAR
"Alexa, add an event on Sunday at 6pm"
"Alexa, do I have any appointments today?"

Productivity

CALENDAR
"Alexa, how many days until the 6th of April?"
"Alexa, link my calendar"
"Alexa, show me my calendar"
"Alexa, what day is it?"
"Alexa, what time is it?"
"Alexa, what's in my calendar for Friday?"
"Alexa, what's in my calendar for next week?"
"Alexa, what's on my calendar tomorrow?"
"Alexa, what's on today?"
"Alexa, what's the date?"

LISTS
"Alexa, add milk to my shopping list"
"Alexa, add a to-do"
"Alexa, create a list"
"Alexa, what's on my shopping list?"
"Alexa, what's on my to-do list?"

OTHER
"Alexa, help me focus" - will suggest a skill to try.
"Alexa, how is traffic to Glasgow?"
"Alexa, is the bank open?"

@tltechsmart

Productivity

REMINDERS
"Alexa, cancel my reminders"
"Alexa, delete my reminder"
"Alexa, remind me again in 10 minutes"
"Alexa, remind me to call Dad in 10 minutes"
"Alexa, remind me to do the laundry at 6pm today"
"Alexa, remind me to feed the dog"
"Alexa, remind me to get groceries tomorrow"
"Alexa, remind me to go to the gym every day at 6pm"
"Alexa, remind me to take my vitamins every day at 8am"
"Alexa, remind me to water the plants every Sunday"
"Alexa, remind me to water the plants"
"Alexa, set a daily reminder"
"Alexa, set a recurring reminder"
"Alexa, set a reminder"
"Alexa, what are my reminders?"

STICKY NOTES
These work best on a device with a screen.
"Alexa, add a sticky note"
"Alexa, create a sticky"
"Alexa, make a sticky note"

TIMERS
"Alexa, cancel my timer?"
"Alexa, how long's left on my timer?"

@tltechsmart

Productivity

TIMERS
"Alexa, set a 40-minute cake timer"
"Alexa, set a chicken timer"
"Alexa, set a cooking timer for 10 minutes"
"Alexa, set a laundry timer for 1 hour"
"Alexa, set a pasta timer for 10 minutes"
"Alexa, set a reading timer for 30 minutes"
"Alexa, set a sleep timer for 20 minutes"
"Alexa, set a workout timer for 20 minutes"
"Alexa, show me my timers?"
"Alexa, what timers do I have set?"

Seasonal

Did you know that Alexa can also help you celebrate those special seasonal occasions?

We've collated a huge list across a range of topics including Christmas, Easter, Halloween, New Year, Other, Pankcake Day and Valentine's Day. We've listed the phrases by category and then by alphabetical order. Let's kick off with Christmas.

CHRISTMAS
"Alexa, am I on the naughty list?"
"Alexa, am I on the nice list?"
"Alexa, ask Santa to read me a letter"
"Alexa, call Santa"
"Alexa, do you like my Christmas jumper?"
"Alexa, do you like my Christmas tree?"
"Alexa, give me Christmas gift ideas"
"Alexa, have I been naughty or nice?"
"Alexa, how many days until Christmas?"
"Alexa, how many sleeps until Christmas?"
"Alexa, how ugly is my Christmas jumper?"
"Alexa, is Santa real?"
"Alexa, Merry Christmas!"
"Alexa, play Christmas music on Amazon Music"
"Alexa, play the top Christmas songs"
"Alexa, show me a Christmas recipe"
"Alexa, sing a Christmas carol"

@tltechsmart

Seasonal

CHRISTMAS
"Alexa, sing a Christmas song"
"Alexa, sing a duet with Santa"
"Alexa, sing Jingle Bells"
"Alexa, tell me a Christmas joke"
"Alexa, tell me a Christmas story"
"Alexa, visit Santa" - opens the Santa Claus skill.
"Alexa, what can you tell me about Santa's reindeer"
"Alexa, what do you know about Rudolph the red-nosed reindeer?"
"Alexa, what's your favourite Christmas movie?"
"Alexa, where is Santa?" - opens the Santa Claus skill.

EASTER
"Alexa, do an Easter rap"
"Alexa, have you seen the Easter bunny?"
"Alexa, how many days until Easter?"
"Alexa, is the Easter bunny real?"
"Alexa, rap about Easter"
"Alexa, tell me an Easter story"
"Alexa, where is the Easter bunny?"

HALLOWEEN
"Alexa, do a Halloween rap"
"Alexa, give me a Halloween hack"
"Alexa, tell me a Halloween joke"

> Bonus Tip: Try saying "Alexa, who is your favourite reindeer?"

@tltechsmart

Seasonal

HALLOWEEN
"Alexa, how many days until Halloween?"
"Alexa, tell me a Halloween story" - plays a story from Amazon Audible.
"Alexa, trick or treat?"
"Alexa, what are you going to dress up as for Halloween?"

NEW YEAR
"Alexa, count down to New Year" - opens the Countdown to New Year skill.
"Alexa, Happy New Year!"
"Alexa, sing Auld Lang Syne"

OTHER CELEBRATIONS
"Alexa, happy Hanukkah"
"Alexa, happy St Patrick's Day"

PANCAKE DAY
"Alexa, what should I have on my pancake?"
"Alexa, what's the best pancake topping?"

VALENTINE'S DAY
"Alexa, be my valentine"
"Alexa, help me write my Valentine's card"
"Alexa, how many days until Valentine's Day?"

@tltechsmart

Seasonal

VALENTINE'S DAY
"Alexa, I love you"
"Alexa, roses are red"
"Alexa, will you be my Valentine?"
"Alexa, will you marry me?"

"Alexa, help me write my Valentine's card"

@tltechsmart

Security/Privacy

In the Getting Started section we provided you with some introductory advice about managing your data. This section provides some further ways that you can customise your Alexa experience, to manage your security and privacy. As usual the commands are listed in alphabetical order for your convenience.

"Alexa, how do I turn off the microphone?"
"Alexa, are you always listening?"
"Alexa, delete everything I said today"
"Alexa, delete what I just said"
"Alexa, do you share my data?"
"Alexa, how do I check my privacy settings?"
"Alexa, how do I see my data?"
"Alexa, how do you protect my data?"
"Alexa, how do you protect my privacy?"
"Alexa, how do you use my data?"
"Alexa, let's talk about privacy"
"Alexa, what are my privacy settings?"
"Alexa, what do you record?"

Smart Home

As you know smart homes is where our passion lies and we'd love to share even more of our smart home know-how, but that would be a whole book in itself!

This section is intended to give you some ideas of where to get started controlling your smart home with your voice.

In many of the examples, you will need to set up compatible smart devices. Look out for the "Works with Alexa" label if you're not sure. Once set up you should be able to connect them to Alexa via the Alexa smartphone app or by saying "Alexa, discover my devices".

We've grouped the commands by topic, which include Heating, Lighting, Routines, Security, etc. Within each list, the commands are provided in alphabetical order.

HEATING
Requires a compatible heating system.
"Alexa, I'm cold"
"Alexa, set the living room to 20 degrees"
"Alexa, set the thermostat to 21 degrees"
"Alexa, turn off the heating"
"Alexa, what's the living room temperature?"
"Alexa, what's the thermostat temperature?"

What can I say to Alexa?

"Alexa, turn on the lights"

@tltechsmart

Smart Home

LIGHTING
Requires a compatible smart bulb, plug or switch.
"Alexa, dim the lights to 50%"
"Alexa, make the living room gold"
"Alexa, turn off the bedroom light"
"Alexa, turn off the lights"
"Alexa, turn on my lights in 30 minutes"
"Alexa, turn on the lights"
"Alexa, turn the lights off in 10 minutes"
"Alexa, turn the lights to soft white"

OTHER
"Alexa, show me my energy dashboard" - opens Loop Energy Saver skill.
"Alexa, show me the baby's room" - connect a compatible camera device to be able to see what's happening in another room.
"Alexa, turn on the fan" - requires a compatible device, or smart plug or switch.
"Alexa, turn on the TV" - requires a compatible Infrared, Radio Frequency remote control converter device (sometimes called an IR/RF Blaster), or smart TV.

@tltechsmart

Smart Home

ROUTINES
We introduced you earlier in the book with some introductory advice and examples for how routines can simplify tasks. To find out more about routines, you can also ask Alexa, just say "Alexa, how do I set up a routine?" or "Alexa, what are smart home routines?"

The best way to set up a new routine is using the Alexa smartphone app. in here you'll find some examples of routines which you can customise or you can make one from scratch.

The examples below will only work if you have created routines with these names.

"Alexa, enable the 'Goodbye' Routine"
"Alexa, enable the 'I'm home' Routine"
"Alexa, enable the 'Morning Shine' Routine"
"Alexa, enable the 'Start my Day' Routine"
"Alexa, start my day"

SECURITY
"Alexa, lock the front door" - requires a compatible device.
"Alexa, show me the front door" - connect a compatible video doorbell to see what's happening outside.

@tltechsmart

Wellbeing

Helping people with their wellbeing was one of our main motivators when we started our own journey of discovering what Alexa can do. It is such a wonderful tool to add to our wellbeing toolkit. In this section you'll find some ideas of things that you can say to your Alexa to boost your wellbeing, all arranged in alphabetical order.

"Alexa, ask Craig David for an affirmation"
"Alexa, give me a healthy living tip"
"Alexa, give me a work from home tip"
"Alexa, give me some relaxation tips"
"Alexa, help me meditate" - opens The Happy Place skill.
"Alexa, help me relax" - opens The Ambient Sounds skill.
"Alexa, help me work out" - opens The Body Coach skill.
"Alexa, how do I keep fit at home?"
"Alexa, how many calories are in a potato?"
"Alexa, play a workout playlist for 10 minutes"
"Alexa, play the playlist 'Workout Pulse' on Amazon Music"

"Alexa, play a sleep playlist for 10 minutes"

@tltechsmart

What can I say to Alexa?

"Alexa, help me work out"

@tltechsmart

What's New

It can be difficult to know what features are available to try on your smart speaker. One way to access this information is to ask about what's new. Although our caviat here is that the information provided may not be what is new, but rather what Amazon has decided that it wants to promote. Never-the-less it could be useful to try asking some of these suggested phrases every so often to see what Alexa suggests.

"Alexa, what are my skills?"
"Alexa, what are your popular skills?"
"Alexa, what are your trending skills?"
"Alexa, what new features do you have?"
"Alexa, what new skills do you have?"

"Alexa, what are your trending skills?"

@tltechsmart

Bonus Skills List

As we mentioned in the section about Skills, it can be difficult to find ones you like. So here is a bonus section with more information about some of our favourite skills on Alexa and what to say to them.

KIDS
Count Dracula - find out how many days it is until Halloween during the month of October. Includes jokes and songs to get you in the Halloween mood.
"Alexa, Open Count Dracula"
"Alexa, ask Count Dracula how many nights till Halloween"

Gruffalo Move - enter the magical world of children's author, Julia Donaldson, with this interactive voice game.
"Alexa, open Gruffalo Move"

Musical Games - play classic kids party games like Musical Chairs, Musical Statues and Musical Bumps.
"Alexa, open Musical Games"
"Alexa, ask Musical Games to play Musical Chairs"

@tltechsmart

Bonus Skills List

LIFESTYLE
Big Sky - real-time weather forecasts for your street address, and locations around the world.
"Alexa, open Big Sky"
"Alexa, ask Big Sky if it will rain"

Bin Calendar - Set up your Alexa to remind you which bin collection is due next whenever you ask.
"Alexa, open Bin Calendar"

Creative Coach - get creative inspiration for projects such as photography, drawing, writing and design.
"Alexa, open Creative Coach"
"Alexa, ask Creative Coach for an idea"

PRODUCTIVITY
Phocus Space - A Pomodoro style timer where you can choose between 25 min or 50 min focus sessions.
"Alexa, open Phocus Space"

SEASONAL
Christmas Countdown - check how many sleeps it is until Christmas and get updates on Santa's preparations for the big day.
"Alexa, open Christmas Countdown"
"Alexa, Ask Christmas Countdown how many sleeps until Christmas"

@tltechsmart

What can I say to Alexa?

"Alexa, open Bin Calendar"

@tltechsmart

Bonus Skills List

Festive Facts - find out random festive facts, like what is the world's tallest Christmas tree, simply by asking Alexa.
"Alexa, open Festive Facts"
"Alexa, ask Festive Facts for a fact"

Seeking Santa - solve a fun filled daily challenge in the 12 days before Christmas.
"Alexa, open Seeking Santa"

WELLBEING
10 Today - Contains a range of exercises designed to be done at home to maintain muscle strength and balance.
"Alexa, open 10 Today"

7-minute Workout - guided exercises designed to increase metabolism, improve energy and lower stress all in just 7 minutes.
"Alexa, open 7 Minute Workout"

Couch to 5K - An easy-to-follow programme to get you off the couch and running for 30 mins (around 5km) in as little as nine weeks.
"Alexa open couch to five k"

@tltechsmart

Bonus Skills List

WELLBEING
Emergency CPR - A five step guide to perform hands-only cardiopulmonary resuscitation (CPR) with a 120 beat per minute audio track.
"Alexa, start emergency c p r"

Easy Yoga - Three different sessions that only take 15mins each. Best for people with a little yoga experience so you can follow the audio instructions.
"Alexa, open Easy Yoga"
"Alexa, ask Easy Yoga for morning yoga"

Kindspace - Check-in daily to measure your wellbeing and take action with wellness tips and activities.
"Alexa, open kind space"
"Alexa, ask kindspace for journaling"

My Scottish Community - Find out more about community groups and activities in your local area and support available nationally. Note: only covers Scotland.
"Alexa, enable my Scottish community"

Sleep Jar - a great app for calming sounds and customisable audio experiences.
"Alexa, open Sleep Jar"
"Alexa, ask Sleep Jar for white noise."

@tltechsmart

CONGRATULATIONS

Next Steps on Your Alexa Adventure

Congratulations! You've unlocked a world of possibilities by mastering the versatile voice commands in this guide. From streamlining daily routines to unlocking entertaining experiences, you now have the power to engage Alexa's capabilities more fully than ever before.

We hope this book has not only equipped you with a comprehensive reference, but also inspired you to explore Alexa's rapidly evolving features with confidence. Don't be afraid to experiment - you may just discover novel ways for your smart speaker to enrich your life.

> The rest of this book is yours to complete, we hope you enjoy your Alexa journey. We've included a few extra cheat sheets and some space to write your own notes.

Remember, this is merely the beginning. As Alexa's abilities continue expanding, we'll be here to support you along the journey to create your perfect home environment. Need assistance? Looking for tips on new features? Our team at TL Tech is just a visit away at www.tltechsmart.com.

@tltechsmart

What can I say to Alexa?

Our mission is to help as many people as possible use technology to have a better quality of life. One way that you can help us is to leave a review about your experience using the book to help others on their technology journey.

@tltechsmart

COMMANDS CHEAT SHEET

General Advice

Start talking with your chosen "wake" word

My wake word is ……………………

Then ask your question or give your instruction

The blue light means Alexa is listening and processing (see more about what each light colour means on the next page)

Basic Commands

To stop or pause: "Alexa, stop" or "Alexa, cancel"
To re-start play: "Alexa, resume" or "Alexa, restart"
To skip a track or song: "Alexa, next"
To change volume: "Alexa, turn down/up the volume" or "Alexa, set the volume to 6"

Things to Try

"Alexa, what day is it?" or "Alexa, what time is it?"
"Alexa, what's happening today?"
"Alexa, what is the weather?"
"Alexa, what's in the news?"
"Alexa, show me my photos"

Video Calling & Dropping In

To answer an incoming call: "Alexa, answer"
To hang up: "Alexa, hang up" or "Alexa, end the call"
To play messages: "Alexa, play messages"

"Alexa, drop in on …………………" or "Alexa, call …………………"

@tltechsmart

LIGHTS CHEAT SHEET   (Page 1 of 2)

Below are the Light Ring/Bar colours you may see on your device and an explanation of what it means.

NO LIGHT: The device is waiting for your commands, either by saying the wake word or pushing the action button.

BLUE with SPINNING LIGHT BLUE: The device is starting up after being powered on or restarted.

BLUE with a LIGHT BLUE LIGHT POINT TOWARD YOU: The device is dealing with your request, after you have asked a question or given an instruction.

BLUE & LIGHT BLUE FLASHING: The device is responding to your request.

RED: The microphone is off or muted. This can be toggled on or off using the mute button on the top of the device.

ORANGE SPINNING: The device is trying to connect to your wireless network.

PURPLE SPINNING: The device has failed to connect to the wireless network. If a restart does not solve this have a look at Amazon's troubleshooting pages for further things to try.

@tltechsmart

LIGHTS CHEAT SHEET (Page 2 of 2)

WHITE: The volume is being adjusted on your device.

BLUE SPINNING TURNING TO SOLID PURPLE WHICH DISAPPEARS TO NO LIGHT: This happens when you enable Do Not Disturb on your device. Note when Do Not Disturb has been enabled you will see no lights so it can be easy to forget you've set it. To disable just say "Alexa, disable Do Not Disturb"

PURPLE: This light will display when interacting with the device to show that Do Not Disturb is turned on.

YELLOW FLASHING: The device has a message or notification waiting for you. Try saying "Alexa, what is my message" or "Alexa, what is my notification".

GREEN FLASHING: There is an incoming call or drop-in. Try saying "Alexa, answer" or "Alexa, ignore".

@tltechsmart

MY NOTES

@tltechsmart

MY NOTES

@tltechsmart

Index

A
accessibility 7, 28
account 30
actions 22-25
alarms 68-69
announcements 31-33
automation 22-25

B
basic commands 29-30, 92
books 38

C
calendars 68-70
calls 31-33
change Alexa voice 28
christmas 73, 86-87
communication 31-33, 92
cooking 11, 64

D
data 5, 77
do not disturb 30
drop in 30, 92

E
easter 74
educational 34-37
emergency help 8, 30
entertainment 38-44
exercise 11, 82, 88-89
explicit lyrics 63

F
farts 51
flash briefing 20
follow-up mode 29

G
games 11, 38, 51-52, 85
getting started 4, 92

H
halloween 74-75
health 82, 89
heating 78
hobbies 64

J
jokes 52-53

K
kids 63, 85

L
launching 10
light ring/bar 5, 93-94
lighting 79
lists 70

M
making a call 31-33, 92
messages 33, 92
music 39-42
mute 30, 93

@tltechsmart

N
new year 75
news 11, 66, 92

P
philsophical questions 53-54
photos 42
podcast 42
poems 54
popular culture 54-57
privacy 5, 77
productivity 68-72, 86
profanity filter 63
profiles 30

R
radio 43
reading 38
recordings 5, 77
relaxing sounds 82, 89
reminders 71
routines 22-25, 81

S
security 5, 77, 81
sending a message 31-33
shopping 66
skills 9-16, 85-89
smart home controls 78-81
smart plug 80

songs by Alexa 48-50
sports 43
sticky notes 71

T
tap to Alexa 7
timers 71-72
transcriptions 5
triggers 22-25
troubleshooting 12, 30
TV 11, 44, 80

V
valentine's 75-76
volume 30, 92, 94

W
wake word 4, 92
weather 66-67, 86, 92
wellbeing 82-83, 88-89
what's new 84
widgets 17-18

@tltechsmart

www.ingramcontent.com/pod-product-compliance
Lightning Source LLC
Chambersburg PA
CBHW050326230526
45471CB00005B/2366